Great Source Dailies™
Student Book

DAILY
Oral Language

Grade
7

Neil J. Vail
Joseph F. Papenfuss

GREAT SOURCE
EDUCATION GROUP
A Houghton Mifflin Company

1

    a. were currently being learned the various mountain ranges and rivers in africa

    b. weve began to study the appalachian mountains but we wont spend to much time learning about that range

2

    a. this here book helping others could of been purchased recently but im not sure

    b. the five boys were whispering and laughing between themselves noone knew that they were planning a entertaining performance

3

    a. derricks father carried the dog home at 930 AM and then he began to bathe it

    b. naomi please get off of that table and set hear by the window

4

    a. if mother is touring the west at kwanzaa shell probably stay in granada hotels

    b. I went to youre apartment yesterday to lend you the short story entitled the tell-tale heart

5

a. on december 2 2000 my father visited st louis to see my sister at washington university

b. because kristen did good at school this year mom is letting her go to france next Fall

6

a. the durham marching band are the better of the four marching groups

b. some of the different drum corps is the beats rattlers and rhythms
i believe

7

a. forrest never had no right to lie his jacket their did he

b. we have broke the worlds record for water skiing on prior lake
in minnesota

8

a. mr grauchets and ms smiths chess scores were good they tied for first place

b. since luisa and karen have arrived they wanted to see the spanish travel magazine

9

a. the class was drove to ninth avenue where they took part in the memorial day parade

b. because the better of the six Parade Floats was one sponsored by the twenty first avenue art association

10

a. our class sometimes go to the school library to read newsweek a magazine of current events

b. mystery theater a popular television series recently put on a play based on a short story called the monkeys paw

11

    a. to understand history better the students have went to see
          shakespeare's play julius caesar

    b. after the play rod and saku were discussing the action when rod said
          i didnt think the romans fighted hard enough

12

    a. irregardless of who wins this game i still think miguel is the best
          of the too players

    b. we bought the following items a stove a tent and three sleeping bags

13

   a. they isnt going down highway 59 i dont think because
of the traffic jam

   b. they gave theirselves a few days to see the brooklyn bridge
and other sights when theyre out east

_____

_____

_____

_____

14

   a. the poem lost land describes the poet's memories of childhood dont it

   b. keiko shouted dawn slid into home plate to win the game for we girls

_____

_____

_____

_____

15

a. grandfather and grandmother went outside of the cabin to see who had stole the corn

b. they decided i think that it had been took by a unknown creature from the forest

16
    a. my brother he dont like to deliver the new york times because its to heavy

    b. there are four girls enjoying the following activities too are reading novels one is typing and one chose to build a tree house

17
    a. because we havent no novel entitled the winds of westbury

    b. we should of planted more bulbs this here Fall father said last monday

18

   a. Shalane complained i was almost froze while watching the movie bicentennial man at the landmark plaza theater

   b. they would of gave more money to the homeless shelter but they didnt have none left

19

   a. i dont want that there teacher to say that the too of you are much to lazy to work.

   b. we grew lots of vegetables this Spring but we should of planted more flowers

20

    a. it rained yesterday and we should of stayed at home instead
        of walking to rock creek park

    b. moms ford have a broke windshield, which the shanahan garage
        will repair on tuesday

21

a. he could of rode with we kids or he might of went with his mom and dad who decided to take the bus

b. lauren dont type good ill be happy too type her letter after ive wrote my own

22

a. sean swum only inside of the lane marker i guess because he aint that good a swimmer

b. kalidia has sang in there church choir more often then dolores has i believe

23

    a. us cheerleaders in this group have wore the same uniforms longer then that there group of cheerleaders

    b. the gentleman who is wearing the blue gray suit works in the university he teaches a course in hindu religion

24

    a. please send the thirty six pound box of books however to 1140 main street palm desert california 92210

    b. hes about to read the song of hiawatha a lengthy Poem by longfellow

25

a. 153 mark twain road
hartford ct
september 7 1999

b. me and my sister are further ahead in our homework than rasheeds brother is

26   a. raul is the better soccer player of the five boys dont you agree

           b. well split the difference, than, between the three of us if that's what
the group want us to do

27   a. nathalie has rode her horse every year in the tri city rodeo
and has never been throwed

           b. before the wrestling team seen the movie marcus had spoke
to the members about there upcoming trip to the east

28

    a. weve wore the same outfits to every game tennis shoes blue trousers and gray shirts

    b. has wayne began reading the short story the necklace in his english Class

29

    a. irregardless of the danger involved in rafting down the cascadia river people still raft down the cascadia river for entertainment

    b. the class therefore will travel to dallas to see the musical the sound of music

30

a. we have plenty of german homework to do before the game begins at 215 PM

b. my uncle he shouted the person who is wearing muddy shoes are dirtying the floor i just cleaned

31

   a. emilio said that he dont want to watch the television series national geographic at his uncles house every week

   b. consuela say them boys hasnt no business teasing her when shes playing soccer in riverview park

32

   a. father has tore the editorial out of the boston globe for me to read but I cant make no sense of it

   b. daryl will you please send a gift subscription to newsweek to youre aunt sheila at 2510 highland blvd in orlando

33

   a. in cooking class ms hidalgo is learning we boys how to prepare
the better salad stew and cookies in the City

   b. friday morning felicia and kyle drawed an cake on the board
to celebrate ms gaudets birthday

34

   a. teresa megan jaret and pedro will go to walt whitman jr high school
to practice singing the battle hymn of the republic

   b. the roads are alright as you travel farther in the State and away
from urban areas i believe

35

    a. lindsey never done no work on her map of europe for prof marinos article landforms of a major continent

    b. many people must of give plenty of thought to the civil rights act, which became law in ad 1965

36

a. the movie the legend of sleepy hollow has came to springfields larger theater because the other theaters dont never have enough seats

b. dont it seem odd that the club has ran over its annual budget already

37

a. every one of them English students have read Milton's long poem paradise lost

b. mrs kitigawa has growed french marigolds from holland but she has gave many of them away two her father and i

38

a. after discussing the issue careful with our lawyers were accusing several Companies of polluting water in lake ontario on the fourth of july

b. ms pelligrini the substitute Teacher brang her notes about the two friends a french short story to class

_____

_____

_____

39

5406 gear avenue
nashville tennessee
june 20 2000
dear enrique
thank you for your invitation
ill be arriving at 730
sincerely
lance

40

a. hes setting down to study machu picchu, a city in the andes mountains
that was discovered in ad 1911

b. miss maria ferraz
271 furber ave
wolfeboro nh

41

a. im sure dr kelley dont never close her office on tower st in january

b. the right rear tire on manuel and bobs toyota busted as they had
almost completed there journey too charleston in the southeast

42

a. mr tatarian didnt no that the fishing club had froze his winning marlin
at central market 5708 vilnia ave

b. jenny and olga isnt really aware that there cake has began to raise
in a open pan

43

a. when she slided down the side of the hill keiko injures her ankle worst then her wrist

b. rosa has threw the football farther then me franco whined

44

a. will carlos leave orin loan a Copy of the eagle of the ninth during september

b. tomas has teached some new songs to the people who sung in the morriston orpheus choir last year i think

45

a. im going to lay down in my room and listen to ricky martin while i right a short letter to my cousin declared tyler

b. buck dont know the names of no poets irregardless of his english teachers efforts in class

46

    a. rogers brother he may of gave a speech in prof velazquezs class about the opera madame butterfly buy puccini

    b. was the well known article hidden from history researched and wrote by karla

47

    a. mr schauss wont you be learning youre students nothing about the battle of agincourt, which takes place in ad 1415

    b. he has spoke about the differences between cells several times in this here biology class

48

a. anna elena and susan havent no reason to set and despair about
the closing of lillys restaurant itll open again next month

b. juan has wore his red white and blue suit every fourth of july
for six years but he has now outgrew it

49

a. when the boys set up camp in yellowstone national park they realized
they had forgot to air out there tent

b. 463 cactus lane
prescott az
may 8 2004

50

a. chantrea has took her bicycle seat to the repair shop otherwise her
father would of throwed it out

b. mr ben hena
64 thunder road
helena mt 59601

51

   a. rachel and aaron went to temple beth-el at 300 PM

   b. i put the latest issue of history today back on the rack after the store
clerk barked this isnt the public library

52

   a. peter would of ate an ham and cheese omelette but he didnt have time
for nothing

   b. last week alicia receives a good grade she wrote her research paper
about baltimore cathedral she wrote her theme good

53

   a. have our swim team ever beat the pentonville cougars at the piccolo sports center

   b. has gov akira left the bill die because he wouldn't sign it

_____

_____

_____

_____

54

8792 shady lane
atkins ar 72723
june 12 2002
dear sonia
thanks for ritas picture itll complete my
photo collection of we mountain climbers
sincerely
christina

55 a. gloria has went for an interview with elsberg electronics i heard

   b. whom has tore my poster its the only antique from the 1964 worlds
      fair that i own

56

a. having wrote my paper i returned the book history of china that
mrs chun borrowed to me on march 18 2003

b. raphael catched up with john rees the tennis instructor
in the restaurant at glendale country club

57

a. the kaibab suspension bridge located in arizona is one of many
suspension bridges in north america

b. dr juanita herrera
832 gaywood street
shreveport la 71102

58

  a. that brooch is one i purchased in sicily with a red stone

  b. the novel an night to remember tells how a british ship struck
      an iceberg said prof agoyo

59

  a. because he was so tired father accidentally spilled maple syrup on sam
      and ramons copy of the constitution

  b. ming sweared that she had wrote her letter to the new york times but
      perhaps she forgot to mail it

60

    a. the bengal Tiger leaped so sudden in the path that the hunters heard theirselves scream with terror

    b. dolores wrote her short story the strange shore while she eats breakfast at a Restaurant on morissey boulevard

61

   a. were going to watch the thanksgiving day parade i think so that we can see representative delgado

   b. it wasnt going to stop raining we lay our tools in the shed beside the cottage at loon lake

62

   a. us kids have sang hanukkah songs many times for the exchange students' club

   b. father had broke a plate he cried i has to many things on my mind

63

    a. i and my friends havent never gave philip and she that chess set
       to play with

    b. on saturday morning luis and me sold thirty seven copies of the
       annapolis capital on duke of gloucester st before lunch time

64

    a. dad has wore the older of them four sweaters for years he thinks
       it is the warmer and more comfortable

    b. because aunt alice has always grew alot of these vegetables
       in her garden peas cabbage and carrots

65

   a. because someone had tore a page out of the book american short
stories i werent able to finish to build a fire the story i wanted to read

   b. i read a exciting Novel about china that was so interesting that i told
my cousin she had to read it

66

    a. my friends they has ate at central park many times they have
        also relaxed at central park often

    b. hasnt the boys never catched any fish or gone swimming
        in the grape river

67

    a. some of my favorite hobbies is painting to cycle and playing soccer

    b. mrs horowitz have you ever went to the blue ridge mountains and saw
        any interesting scenery

68

a. there is two many commas in youre paragraph, karen however i think this is the better organized paragraph you have ever wrote

b. my Social Studies teacher learned me that south america is located among the atlantic and pacific oceans

69

a. them bottles of milk on the porch might bust if the temperature drops below freezing sit them in the kitchen

b. the mail carrier delivered the may issue of preservation magazine at 1045 AM

70

a. the street lights on west blvd is broke we cant see nothing their

b. please read the poem matty groves and then describe the characteristics of ballads

71

    a. when i was in the north last august i visited a ancient house with
          a interesting past

    b. didnt youre English teacher learn you nothing about the major themes
          in the novel robinson crusoe

72

    a. dad shaked the box and said there's no way of knowing what is inside

    b. will the national librarian council meeting be held in dallas texas
          next month

73   a. the institute of cooking is located on haussman blvd in topeka kansas i believe

        b. that there exmayor of our city has spoke to the urban gardeners club recently within the last few weeks

74   a. their seems to be frequent accidents at them too factories on lagrange street

        b. them too have fighted and argued since nursery school its best for them boys to be kept apart

75

a. 4793 gina drive
   appleton wa
   february 20 2004

b. did coleridge the english Poet right the long poem the rime
   of the ancient mariner

76

   a. omar observed the department of public works has began to restore the park on the other side of hartman road

   b. has he ever ran and then did push-ups at the holland park sports center

77

   a. the exercises ms pacheco has gave us to finish cover these punctuation points colons quotation marks and question marks

   b. aunt lupita has took this here medicine for many years and swears she hasnt never had a fever

78 a. irregardless of his skill at dancing chuck goes to astaire dance studios
      every tuesday thursday and saturday to practice

  b. mrs lorraine hope
     5079 north franklin street
     st. louis mo 63133

79   total power industries
      876 linden road
      denver co 80202
      dear sir or madam
      please replace part #79463 thank you
      sincerely

80

a. we saw the play the crucible when it was in our local theater
   we enjoyed watching it

b. the children had drank the whole gallon of milk and i had to go
   to consumers supermarket to by some more

81   a. the antiques roadshow hasnt began yet tv guide must have listed
it incorrectly at 730

       b. when were finished with this homework i and sonia will help
lennox and he complete there assignment

82   a. many of the great moslem mosques of north africa was built
at the same time that christians were building cathedrals
during the middle ages

       b. havent youre friends never brung you any souvenirs
from a vacation

83

a. nomar asked me to borrow him my bicycle pump but i told
him i had broke it

b. serena remarked because the police found my dog ruffles
on the corner of dean and highway 78

84

a. mom remarked if alex had not rose the temperature in the refrigerator
the lemonade would of froze

b. me and my Aunt seen a model of the titanic at jakes hobby shop

85   a. me and francesca have took our reports about the happy prince an English short story to class

        b. has ayeesha threw away that there brush that is different from the ones that we paint with in Art class

86

a. there was six guests trapped inside there rooms in the burning victoria hotel however firefighters breaked there doors down and rescued them

b. us students visited washington dc last fall consequently we were able to see the lincoln memorial

87

a. ms palmeiro is it true that the eiffel tower was once the taller building in the world

b. henry wadsworth longfellow wrote the poem paul revere's ride he was an american author

88   a. my Parents have gave me and my sister books sweaters and posters

           b. them kids have drew sketches of potomac school for an art assignment i believe

89   a. we have ate at sandys restaurant many times sandy's restaurant is near our house

           b. my friends went to see the movie et but i couldnt go so i decided to walk around the city

90

a. at one time the overland limited is the finer and more popular passenger train in the united states preston remarked

b. i laid down at 1000 PM but father set up writing until 1245 AM

91

    a. me and grandpa catched thirty two trout in the pools near mt baldy

    b. dad said he should of wrote a postcard to your uncle in africa

92

    a. i seen mr jimenez buy these items at the hardware store some sandpaper a scraper and a brush

    b. as we were setting in the tiptree motor lodge governor malone strolls in

93

    a. did you chose the largest of the too pineapples at the shop on ferndale blvd

    b. i want to learn you about the golden age of greece, the period between 477–431 bc

94

    a. one of the boys aren't going to read no novel called war and peace

    b. they have ate at health food haven before and they have always been happy with the menu

95
   a. because there is far too many <u>verys</u> in youre essay

   b. hiking through the north many species of flowers different
       from those in the south were seen by us

96

    a. at citrus park father shaked an orange tree and twenty three oranges fell off of the branches

    b. no mom hasnt spoke to our neighbors about joining us at the palisades restaurant for dinner next week

97

    a. The Ambassador from venezuela as i suspected knowed that the submarine neptune had sank

    b. 8754 parley road
brattleboro vt
july 16 2003

98

   a. at st stephens hospital i read the short story fame game this short story
       was in the magazine literature review

   b. my little sister left me help her with the ws she was practicing

_____

_____

_____

_____

99

   a. my brother dont have no glue to complete his wooden model
       of a hindu temple

   b. yes the mail carrier she delivered too letters and gives me a postcard

_____

_____

_____

_____

100

a. his grandfather may of drove a tank in the korean war but im not certain

b. i addressed the package to mr evan jones at 683 palm street tallahassee florida he just moved their

101

a. last fall me and mom leaved for new york and drove on the new jersey turnpike most of the way

b. reggie has lent that map of the battle of yorktown from me before he don't have a copy of his own

102

a. we have swam at vanderbilt park many times it always seems to crowded

b. me and my cousins traveled to boston massachusetts but we dont visit the ship the constitution

103   a. yes the chicago tribune reported that many people have fleed from cuba

          b. i have took the bitter tasting cough syrup but i have not drank the hot tonic

104   a. father did you telephone dr chavez at 200 AM

          b. she dont recall nothing important about the poem the seasons, which was wrote in the eighteenth century

105

a. the Lion run to the edge of the rocks then it sprung across the ravine

b. a aging poster inside of the theatre advertised the barker brothers circus

106

   a. hasnt gustavo brung back that volume you borrowed him of the book
the call of the wild

   b. they have always drove out west for christmas rather than take
the trailways bus theyre

107

   a. because she knowed that governor kelley wouldnt rise
the minimum wage

   b. i throwed the frisbee toward blair rd however it didnt spin
the write way

108
   a. no trees no way can grow on top of the capitol carmen remarked

   b. the students theirselves begun to raise enough money to see the movie anna and the king

_____

_____

_____

109
   a. the self appointed expert rung our doorbell to see if we had read his Article are the cities reviving

   b. at filmore and second yesterday a boy played the Violin good

_____

_____

_____

110

a. the soil had froze and then we lose our enthusiasm digging
the foundation

b. mom said that it was alright for i and dana to visit lightning valley
our favorite place to ski

111

   a. them students havent no time to watch that sports today program
       on television

   b. yes while she was at clivedon middle school my sister she had drew
       a picture of sunbathers laying beside a pool

112

   a. mrs kato asked have you ever rode down st cecilia avenue
       in a mercedes

   b. the australians we met in quebec last march were friendly
       violetta observed

113

   a. my grandparents have gave me these here chores sitting the table
      to wash the dishes and rake the leaves

   b. no i havent never sang america the beautiful at a assembly

114

   a. i still havent broke the track record i was five seconds to slow

   b. the early music ensemble wont perform in hartford one
      of the musicians has broke their wrist

115

a. leaping for the basketball the net was grabbed by the player yesterday at hanson stadium

b. me and tonya thinks that our parents strawberry plants are the healthier on our block

116   a. last spring by the way prof maia flew across the pacific ocean
           from los angeles to tokyo to study japanese traditions

        b. rushing in from the street a box was dropped by the boy on the stairs

117   a. my uncle lives at 832 viking ln portland maine which
           is in the northeast

        b. at 1000 this morning mom asked have the workers came
           to lie the paving stones yet

118   a. im planning to take my cat weebis to the vet's this saturday
irregardless of the expense

b. tainas cousin has fell and tore her stockings alot recently

119   a. if he had taught carlos the lyrics he could of sang in the choir

b. after three weeks at the philadelphia fair i was relieved
to be home again

120

a. mike was able to clean the apartment and washing the dishes however he doesnt finish the laundry

b. victor had a choice either to visit carplaza mall or taking a boat ride on lake michigan

121

a. the andes span several countries in south america ms canesco remarked as she unrolled the map

b. yes our teacher learned us that william blake wrote the long poem the french revolution

122

a. isnt them foreign students going to stay at the roundup hotel in reno when they tour the west

b. this here palm plant has growed to large for your apartment it took up two much room in the kitchen

123

    a. me and my cousin has chose to visit the metropolitan museum
of art to see the art of the french renaissance

    b. my aunts coat comes from filenes a department store
with the velvet trim

124

    a. would you like to read the jungle book or should i borrow it to
consolata

    b. why we have knew for weeks that alot of students would want there
pictures taken at the variety show

125   4986 belmont avenue
        portland or 97208
        april 6 2001
        dear vinny
        well see you this weekend we hope
        your cousin
        chuck

126

   a. have you ever spoke to mrs rubinstein about a donation for the jimmy fund—the one you were to have ask for last week

   b. me and her doesnt know how to begin our article that we want to send to science illustrated

127

   a. the rain had stopped sudden at 130 PM we went back to the baseball field

   b. my brother he hasnt said nothing to father about the plate it is broken

128

a. the workers have slow began to restore the older of the four Victorian house on carolina avenue

b. inside of the garden we seen an orange tree we shaked the orange tree for oranges

129

a. martina has youre father left you put youre savings in the tiptree bank yet asked preston

b. mr. ahmed told us that the state religion of england which is anglicanism begin when henry viii broke away from roman catholicism

130   a. he may of did his homework—memorizing the poem ode to liberty

        b. get away from that there shed and come hear at once mom yelled

131

   a. sitting for hours in traffic on highway 95 many people must long
for the return of trains i think

   b. hes going to the carlisle public library to collect information about
the battle of hastings, which was a battle that took place in England
in the eleventh Century

132

   a. we lent the following items for our vacation in yellowstone national
park too backpacks a tent and a stove

   b. before 800 on weekday mornings i usually swim for forty five
minutes in our local pool

133

a. the article visiting britain mentions the cutty sark at greenwich london which is anchored there

b. after we left home at 530 PM we walked to the grub street inn then we drunk some lemonade

134

a. havent you read nothing in the virginia pilot about the accident on jefferson rd and mansfield dr

b. me and my cousin wont attend them too girls party instead well go to the lowell folk festival

135

a. at 715 AM mom seen the smallest of them too huskies that bark
to much

b. at the getty museum she seen a landscape by leon kossoff
a modern british painter

136

   a. on the fourth of july mayor denham read passages from the book
founding father to the audience

   b. My raleigh ten speed bike needs many new parts given to me
by my grandparents

137

   a. the boys theirselves have began painting mr santanders house
at 873 burroughs road

   b. terance have you threw them old magazines away yet asked aunt
mamie

138   a. i have taught my cousin in memphis thirty three wrestling positions but he dont remember alot of them

       b. mom has drove along atherton avenue many times looking for that there store called milk and honey

139   a. my uncle he brung me the larger of the four fruit bars that had froze on the back porch

       b. us students finished quick and then a new task was given to us by ms polonia

140

a. on rainy days i like reading to listen to the soundtrack from the movie grease and painting

b. yoko she went sailing then she went jogging with her friends then she came home for supper

141

   a. i have took the television that i broke to fair repairs a store on toledo drive

   b. gazing out the window at home in albany the clouds looked heavy and threatening

142

   a. because they could of ate at that there thai restaurant last winter

   b. we havent never rode to herring cove beach to lay in the sun but perhaps we should do that next week

143

   a. luisa has gave i and my sisters a catalog from a store at 7351 overland road topeka kansas which we find interesting

   b. since we havent no butter mom has went to tonis convenience store

144

   a. me and my cousins can take the younger of the three visitors and introduce them to my little brother

   b. fabio said a documentary about the rolling stones appeared on television before the simpsons

145

a. i think that each of these wires have a function but im not sure
what each one of those wires do

b. were taking the bus downtown to meet friends to eat lunch and
a movie might be a good place for us to go

146

a. watermelons have been growed for many years by my parents
which are the largest on hudson lane

b. ms gomez is going to take us to the following plays the tempest
macbeth and king lear

147

a. mr beckman learned them students german on mondays
and wednesdays at brookside junior high school

b. father asked have you tore those pants that you worn
for the first time on thursday

148

  a. irregardless of the storm yolanda wants to cross the mississippi river to see arsenal island

  b. uncle kordell have gave i and ed some advice and then we baited our hooks quite good and then we cast our lines

149

  a. oscar luttati an ex football star has sang in this church and he had been christened here

  b. miss ishigure asked doesnt you never get tired of mowing the lawn

150

a. him and landon have to complete the project by friday march 8 or theyll not receive no grades

b. shalane said i have came to the beach to lay in the sun and not to set in a tidal pool

151

   a. in the himalaya mountains of asia the indians rise cashmere goats
for there fleece

   b. yes mr olson has spoke to barry and i about the makeup used
in the movie the wizard of oz

152

   a. yesterday father says that he wished that he had growed up in the west
before the gold rush

   b. i knowed that moms decision was final she would not leave my rabbit
hopper live inside of my room

153

   a. mary beth hasnt never as i recall went to goldsmith college to see the play a raisin in the sun

   b. hiking wrestling and to swim is the hobbies i enjoy more

154

   a. the Magician in front of the japanese screen vanished as mysterious as she had appeared

   b. us five girls done the construction work between ourselves no boys would help us

155

a. ms. Perez told us that the poem death at sea tells about a ship that
sunk during the golden age of greece

b. aunt delia called at 600 PM she called because she wanted to thank
my brother and i for righting to her

156

   a. the Collie is my favorite breed of dog it has a long thin face and we has four of them

   b. the world religions study club has began planning a trip to philadelphia pennsylvania to visit the tibetan buddhist center an organization that welcomes all people

157

   a. last night father he was angry with me because i had drank claras juice by mistake

   b. them children couldnt watch teletubbies at 700 on saturday morning mom had took the television set to guerrero electronics for repair

158

a. yesterday marco lended me his goggles and i went to clearwater lake and swum

b. my cousins bedroom overlooks flowerhill golf course the bedroom has a built in stereo system

159

a. because them boys i believe were nominated to the all state soccer team last week

b. ms irene potter
7826 holden street
provo ut

160

a. isnt me and rita supposed to help clean the kitchen and washing moms car

b. irregardless of my friends advice to him raheim decided to by the old buick and trying to fix it

161   a. them tourists must of ate at piazza navona a restaurant
on berkeley road

      b. eric lost the book about california that mrs ferraro gived him
last thursday

162   a. walking home from the burnham county harvest festival on route 1a
three creatures were saw by us a skunk a raccoon and a possum

      b. uncle marcel brung my brother and i a model of the normandie
a french ship

163

a. us boys were almost froze watching the musical cats at bryant park last night

b. mrs nerudas one strawberry plant dont have no strawberries on it yet mom remarked

164

a. yes we believe that youre bicycle is better then mine in several ways

b. mrs wong my Social Studies teacher explained that two many verys was in my report about the october revolution in russia

165

a. my father he almost felled off of his chair when i said i want to take judo lessons

b. hearing the backdoor slam the book was lain down by the girl

166

a. the vienna philharmonic orchestra a long time popular favorite was scheduled for a Concert in symphony hall

b. alicia asked if the characters in the novel only the lonely didnt remind me of them in the short story the suburbs

167

a. last week we went to kristof's kitchen on churchill ave we have ate there frequently

b. hasnt dr mussina learned you nothing about protecting youre skin from the sun

168   a.   in our english class the one taught by mr corvey we have been
assigned to read the long poem beowulf

   b.   yes i may of broke a record last christmas when i built
a ten foot high snowman

169   a.   shes setting in her room trying to decide how many os their
is in kalamazoo

   b.   my uncle he has rode on the lightning express thirty four times
he likes trains

170

a. aunt roberta wasnt sure to who she would give the most valuable of the too paintings

b. we went in the museum on fifth ave. to see an old volume of dantes book the divine comedy the work was wrote in the fourteenth century

171   a. my mother said me and youre cousin seen the new type of jet
at the leonardo da vinci airport outside of rome

          b. calvin hasnt growed nothing in his garden this year he was
in memorial hospital last spring

172   a. after we had took the arrowheads and pottery out of the soil we lay
them on the ground spread them out and washing them

          b. because we had flew to cleveland ohio we werent able to attend
youre sisters wedding

173 a. in its religion section religious life magazine featured a article about the influence of buddhism on japanese culture

b. our club is going to tomkin park to play football eat lunch and will go hiking

174 a. during hanukkah for the past too years our club visits graceland retirement home

b. i have broke the larger of the six jars that have set on that there table for weeks

175   a. because of the record high temperatures i haven't wore this sweater
          I received from my grandfather

       b. dont guernica a famous anti-war painting hang in the prado
          in madrid spain

176

   a. dad and me have caught many fish in wallowa lake wallowa lake is located in Eastern oregon near enterprise

   b. damian has wrote an article for the morning telegraph entitled global warming and this article should appear in mondays edition

---

177

   a. marjorie and i want to go hiking if it dont rain

   b. after dr millier had ate lunch he set down to read the short story the distant cry

---

---

178   a. all season motors on clasemont road have some cheap fords which
           I seen last saturday

       b. renalda dont think that october 8 2000 was the day when the mannix
           corporation begun business

_____

_____

_____

179   a. there is some people in the sea islands of south carolina who
           speak gullah a language that may have originated in africa

       b. them there boys have sang in the grace chapel boys choir
           for many years

_____

_____

_____

180 a. because my cousin learned portuguese good and now he wants
to spend a year in portuguese speaking são paulo brazil

b. my uncle has chosen to take us to washington dc when our new
senator is swore in